Lewis Grizzard
on Fear of Flying*

*"Avoid pouting pilots and
mechanics named Bubba."*

Published by
LONGSTREET PRESS, INC.
2150 Newmarket Parkway
Suite 102
Marietta, Georgia 30067

Printed in the United States of America

1st printing, 1989

Library of Congress Catalog Number 88-083933

ISBN 0-929264-21-5

This book was printed by R. R. Donnelley and Sons, in
Harrisonburg, Virginia. The text type was set in ITC Clear-
face Regular by Typo-Repro Service, Inc., Atlanta, Georgia.
Cover and book design by Chandler & Levy Design, Inc.,
Atlanta, Georgia.

Lewis Grizzard
on Fear of Flying

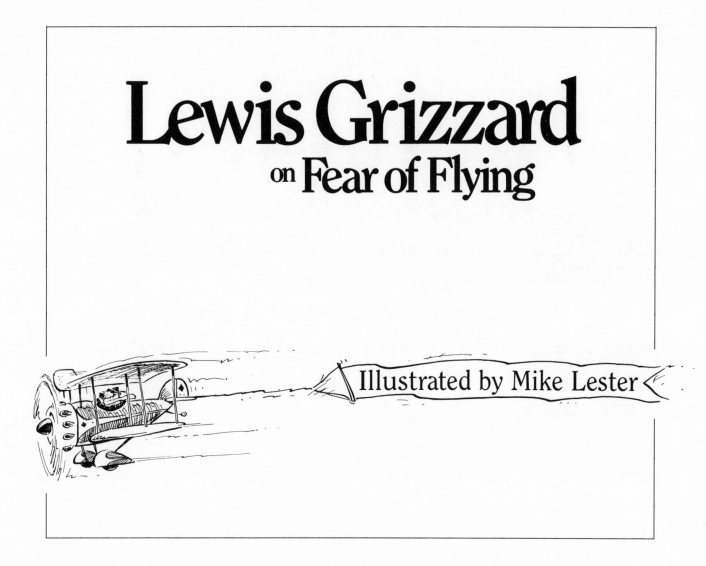

Illustrated by Mike Lester

Longstreet Press
Atlanta, Georgia

Also by Lewis Grizzard

Don't Bend Over in the Garden, Granny,
You Know Them Taters Got Eyes

When My Love Returns from the Ladies Room,
Will I Be Too Old to Care?

My Daddy Was a Pistol and I'm a Son of a Gun

Shoot Low, Boys—They're Ridin' Shetland Ponies

Elvis Is Dead and I Don't Feel So Good Myself

If Love Were Oil, I'd Be About a Quart Low

They Tore Out My Heart and Stomped That Sucker Flat

Don't Sit Under the Grits Tree with Anyone Else But Me

Won't You Come Home, Billy Bob Bailey?

Kathy Sue Loudermilk, I Love You

Contents

Consider, if you will, the adjective *flighty*, meaning foolish or silly. Now consider its source, the noun *flight*, meaning the act of moving through space. See the connection? This could have been a very short book.

My editor, however, is not a well man. In fact, he considers a fill-up at the gas station as a long-term investment. So rather than have some hysterical widow call me at all hours of the night, I've decided to present my whole case. Flight attendants, please secure the cabin for takeoff.

Winging It

For thousands of years men have wanted to fly. The early Greeks and Romans, many of whom were a little light in their sandals anyway, put wings on their gods to make them seem superior. What they actually did was create the first drag queens.

In the Middle Ages, men of science tried to recreate bird wings. They strapped their devices onto the shoulders of daredevils and found a tall cliff. Within a hundred years, daredevils were almost extinct.

Hot-air balloons were the rage in the late 1800s, but they had serious navigational problems. A fellow in Boston trying to visit his girl in Quincy could catch a bad breeze and wind up having dinner with the lobsters.

Finally in the early 1900s, a couple of bicycle repair-men, Wilbur and Orville Wright, kept a flying machine

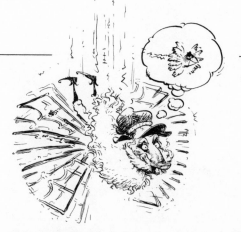

aloft for less time than it takes to find a Hare Krishna at the airport, but that was long enough.

The Age of Flight was born.

Unfortunately, The Age of Safe Landings was another couple of years away. Seems that Wilbur and Orville spent all their time worrying about going up and neglected to consider the problem of coming down.

My great-great uncle, Alton Aloysius Grizzard, was at Kill Devil Hill, North Carolina, that day. He is the one you see in the historic pictures holding a sign that reads, "If God had intended for man to fly, He would have made the wheel square." Uncle Alton was the first (and last) activist

in our family. Anyway, he said that when that flying machine hit the ground, pieces went everywhere. "There was so much broken wood, they didn't have to split kindling for a month. And poor Orville, he was skint from his nose to his toes. It was an awful sight," is how Uncle Alton described the crash to the family.

From that time on, whenever Grizzards gathered for any occasion, they always told the story of Uncle Alton, the first flight, and the first crash. Years later, when the state of North Carolina adopted as its motto "First in Flight," Uncle Alton led a movement to make them also say "First in a Heap." Truth in advertising, he called it. Pissing in the wind, my daddy called it.

It was into that climate that I was born on October 20, 1946—the same day a cropduster crashed into Skeeter Jordan's chicken house and wiped out 1,347 hens. The family said it was an omen. Skeeter said it was a mess.

Rooted in Iron

I grew up with a passionate love for trains. Any psychiatrist would say that hearing the story about the first plane crash over and over was responsible for that love. But in my case, it was deeper than that. It was at my very core.

When I was full grown, which coincided more or less with the *Roots* craze, it occurred to me that I didn't know the details about my birth. I don't mean what time of day, or how long the labor was, or what color gloves the doctor wore. I mean the actual circumstances under which I was conceived.

Since my father was a serviceman who enjoyed the spirits, I knew there was a possibility that I would be told, "Well, one night your father came home loaded and . . ."

In fact, it was much more romantic than that. According to my mother, who spared me the details, she and my

father were on a train, headed home after a long separation. Somewhere south of Atlanta, as the crack *Man o' War* rode the Central of Georgia high iron, my parents broke the ground that spawned me.

Shortly after this discovery, a young lady in a bar asked what sign I was born under. I said, "If you consider the moment of conception as the actual date of first life, I may have been born under a sign that read, 'Dining Car in Opposite Direction.'"

No Reel Models

As a kid, I was never all that impressed by airplanes. My dad was a foot soldier, so I never heard stories of aerial combat. The planes that flew over our town weren't much to see—mostly military cargos that looked like Greyhound Scenic cruisers with wings. And, of course, every time a plane went over, somebody brought up Uncle Alton.

Even in the movies and on television, flying wasn't all that hot. Peter Pan, who could fly all over the room, was too swishy for my tastes. I didn't know anything about sexual persuasion in those days, but I knew a fruitcake when I saw one. Maybe it would have been different if Mickey Rooney had played the role instead of Mary Martin.

Superman had everything going for him except one thing—he would never stand up to Lois Lane. That bimbo

led him around like she had a Kryptonite collar on him. I couldn't stand to see him leap tall buildings in a single bound and then hop every time she called.

And what a disappointment Batman was. That sucker

wore a cape like Superman, but he couldn't have flown if they had bought him a ticket. And Robin, with his bird legs, was just as bad; he'd have been better off eating worms and rock, rock, rockin' along.

Mighty Mouse? Ever notice how he flew in to save the day only *after* the bad guys had beaten the pulp out of some little fellow? An ounce of prevention may be worth a pound of cure in the real world, but it wasn't worth its weight in cheese in TV ratings.

And then there was Sky King and his ugly niece, Penny, the one with the Ovaltine mustache. All Sky ever did with his plane was round up stray cows. Heck, Lassie could do that without ever leaving the ground.

So there just weren't a lot of role models who glorified flying for me. Trains, on the other hand, were the talk of the old men I knew growing up. And there was that soft spot in my daddy's heart for trains.

The Train Gang

Trains were always so romantic, especially their names. I often rode the *Nancy Hanks* between Atlanta and Savannah on the Central of Georgia Line. Later I took the *Silver Comet* from Atlanta to Washington and the *Southern Crescent* to New Orleans.

Once on the *Zephyr* from Chicago to San Francisco, I met an Italian fellow in the club car. He spoke very little English and I spoke no Italian. I did, however, manage to get his name and to ask, "What do you do for a living in Italy?"

"I am a painter," Oscar said.

See how romantic? Have you ever had a drink with an Italian artist, somewhere between Denver and Cheyenne, Wyoming, while traveling in an airplane?

"And what do you paint?" I asked my new Italian friend.

"Landscapes? Still lifes? Portraits?"

"Houses," Oscar answered. "I am house painter."

OK, so how many Italian house painters have you ever met on an airplane?

I met two middle-aged women traveling from Louisville to Chicago.

"The train is the only way to fly," said one.

"It's the *only* way I'll fly," laughed her companion.

They sat in the lounge car talking and drinking beer for a couple of hours. I watched them have at least six beers each. When the train reached Chicago, they were flying higher than anybody else on the train.

Another time I witnessed an older man join an older lady in the lounge-car booth next to mine. The old boy immediately started sweet-talking her.

"I haven't had any men friends since my husband, Mr. Willoughby, died," she said.

"Don't worry, honey," answered the man. "I'm too old to be dangerous, just still young enough not to realize it."

They were holding hands by the time I went to my sleeping compartment. I'm convinced there was still some clickety in both their clacks.

A New Line of Worry

I held out against airplanes for years, but finally the travel demands of my profession forced me to begin flying. In the old days, a book publisher would call and say, "Could you be in Bakersfield, California, by Friday?" He would be calling on the previous Saturday.

"Certainly," the author would answer. "I can connect with the *Super Chief* in Chicago and be there in plenty of time."

But book publishers and the rest of the business world don't operate in such a civil manner anymore. Now they say, "Can you be in Bakersfield by five this afternoon?" He's calling at ten in the morning. And the author is expected to answer, "No problem. I'll shave and shower and catch the noon flight, and with the time change, I'll have time to get a haircut in the L.A. airport."

1958   1988

   I either had to start flying or find a new line of work. I
checked with the owner of the neighborhood liquor store,
but he didn't need any help. Same thing at the gas station.
I had two choices: become a street person or learn to fly. I
never did like sleeping outdoors.

The Wild Blue Yonder

It was fear at first flight.

If my first experience had been on a big jet, it might not have been so bad. I mean, there's more room inside those things than in my first house. But my inaugural flight was on a small prop plane en route to a football game.

I first suspected I was in trouble when the same woman who sold me the ticket also loaded the baggage and then piloted the plane. The second tip-off was that all the seats were folding chairs bolted to the floor; they even said Samsonite across the back. When we took off, I saw fire shooting out of the engines, and the plane shook more than the curvaceous Kathy Sue Loudermilk on a hayride. I squeezed the chair arms so tightly that the plastic handles molded to my grip. I held my breath until my eyes bugged, but I decided that going down in a fiery crash

was no worse than literally exploding in mid-air.

Half an hour into the flight, the pilot turned to me and asked, "Want something to eat?"

"Yeah, I guess so," I said, surprised that a meal would be served on such a short flight.

She handed me an apple and a pocketknife. "Just cut off what you want and pass it to the fellow behind you," she said.

Shortly afterwards, we hit an air pocket and my head hit the ceiling. What I mean is that the plane dropped about ten feet in a second, while everything on the inside stayed where it was. If the apple had slowed down enough passing my mouth, I'm sure I would have thrown it up, but it went directly to my skull and splattered there.

I got off the plane weak-kneed and lily-livered. Uncle Alton was right. From then on, every flight was a challenge.

Safety in Numbers

Let me clear up one misconception: I actually am not afraid of flying. It's the prospect of crashing and burning to a crisp that scares me.

"That's silly," said a stewardess friend. "Statistically speaking, you're safer in an airplane than in an automobile."

I don't buy that. Anything that goes five hundred miles per hour and they make you strap yourself inside can't be all that safe. Besides, if an automobile develops a problem with the engine, you just pull off the road and park it. Try pulling an airplane into the emergency lane when the engines overheat.

"I've almost done that, too," said the friend. "I was in a two-engine prop, and we lost power in both engines. We were directly over Palm Beach, Florida, so we just glided in for a safe landing."

Nothing to it. But engines don't always go out over Palm Beach. Try gliding into the Rockies sometime.

Another friend used a different statistical approach. "More people die from slipping in their bathtubs than in commercial airplane crashes," he said.

"If there's any way I can travel in a bathtub, I'm willing to take my chances," I answered.

There's lots to be afraid of about flying. For example, why is it that the first word you see when you arrive at an airport is *Terminal*? Couldn't they call it something else?

Why must stewardesses always point out, "Your seat cushion may be used as a flotation device"? A flotation device! If I had wanted to float to Dallas, I would have chartered a canoe.

A Rear View

I read an article in a magazine about a stewardess who had survived two plane crashes. Imagine going back up again if you were lucky enough to survive a crash; somebody ought to count her cards. Her advice to air travelers was simple: "If you're ever in an 'emergency situation' (that means going down in flames over the Atlantic), don't panic."

Right, I'll just sit there and wait for cabin service to be resumed.

I asked a pilot friend what advice he would offer to anyone in an "emergency situation."

"I've flown thousands of hours," he said. "If anything happens to the plane or there are signs of trouble, I advise the following: Bend down as far as you can behind the seat in front of you. Grab each ankle securely. Place your head

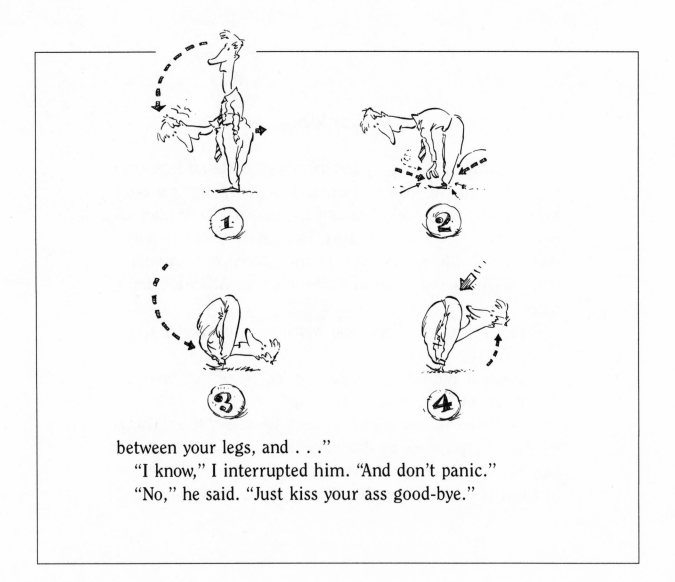

between your legs, and . . ."

"I know," I interrupted him. "And don't panic."

"No," he said. "Just kiss your ass good-bye."

Sunday Services

I was sitting on a plane one Sunday afternoon recently, waiting for the last of the baggage to be loaded. I looked out my window to the ground below and saw an old boy in blue jeans and a work shirt with a big wrench in his hand. Embroidered on his breast pocket was "Bubba" and under that "Maintenance Department."

Now, where I come from, fellows named Bubba with big wrenches in their hands work on '57 Chevys, not on jet airliners. And folks who work on Sunday are at the bottom of the seniority list, which means they don't have a lot of experience.

I watched Bubba scratch for a minute, then reach up with his wrench and tighten something. Or loosen something. I reached for the air sickness bag.

Fire Patrol

The episode with Bubba really scared me, so I decided to do some investigation into airplane maintenance. I set up an interview with Ernest P. Slipshod, chief mechanic and propeller twirler for Wingandaprayer Airlines, whose home office is in an abandoned warehouse in Crowflies, Mississippi. Their company motto is painted across the front of the warehouse: "Come Fly with Us—We'll Take a Chance If You Will."

"Mr. Slipshod," I began, "can you say that you and your mechanics are doing a good job of making certain that Wingandaprayer's planes are always airworthy?"

"Is this going to be on television?" Mr. Slipshod asked.

I assured him that it was for a book I was writing, not for the evening news.

"Good, 'cause if it was," he said, "I wanted to change

my shirt. I got one of them shirts in back that's got my name sewn over the pocket. Says right there on my shirt, 'Ernest P.' They give me that shirt special last year after I put out the fire."

"What fire?" I quickly asked.

"It wasn't nothing, really," said Mr. Slipshod. "Some of the pilots were cuttin' up in the cockpit over Hattiesburg, and while the navigator was asleep, they give him a hotfoot."

"You mean they lit fire to the navigator's shoes?"

"Yeah, some of our pilots got a real good sense of humor. The navigator didn't think it was all that funny, though, so he got out his cigarette lighter and lit one of the pilot's hair. When they landed, I had to jump in the cockpit and stomp out all the flames. I wasn't able to save the navigator's shoe, but I did put the pilot's hair out.

Course, he had these recurring headaches for months. I had to stomp pretty hard to get his hair to stop smoldering."

"Didn't the passengers get nervous during all these hijinks?" I asked.

"There was this one fellow that got all bent out of shape and said he was going to sue us, but Bobby Earl, my assistant, hit him upside the head with a wrench, and we didn't hear no more from him after that."

"Mr. Slipshod," I continued, "do you check the engines on all the airplanes regularly?"

"Check 'em every Fourth of July whether they need checkin' or not."

"I see. And do you do this personally?"

"Not every time, 'cause I'm really busy with the Shriners. But there ain't nothing Bobby Earl can't fix when he's sober."

"Bobby Earl sometimes drinks on the job?"

"Not a lot," answered Mr. Slipshod. "Oh, he might have a couple of six packs while he's tightenin' up a few loose screws, but he's still the best one-eyed mechanic I ever saw."

I asked Mr. Slipshod where he had trained to become an airline mechanic.

"Took me one of them correspondence courses back in the fifties. I saw this ad in a magazine that said, 'Be a chief airline mechanic or lawn mower repairman in sixty days or less.' I sent in three hundred dollars and they sent me this book on what makes airplanes fly. I was in business."

"Are you proud, Mr. Slipshod, of Wingandaprayer's safety record?" I asked.

"Dang right," he said proudly. "Three out of every five flights we got makes it."

Halfway Home

You think I'm kidding? Well, if you don't believe that fact is stranger than fiction, try this one on:

Late last year, a jet airliner landing in Pensacola, Florida, broke in half. I mean, one half of the plane came almost totally unattached from the other half.

Can you just imagine what the pilot told the boys back in flight headquarters?

"Had a little trouble down in Pensacola, chief."

"Yeah? What happened?"

"The plane broke in half."

"Do what?"

"Well, chief, it sort of came apart at the hinges. But we got the ground crew out there now trying to glue it back together."

You hardly ever hear about a bus or train breaking in

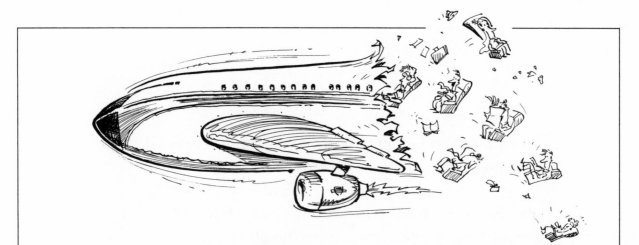

half. Even as much trouble as they had with Corvairs and Mavericks, I don't remember an instance where one of them broke in half.

The obvious next question is, if your plane is going to break in half, which part is safest to sit in? The smart money says sit in the back because no plane ever *backed* into a mountain.

All I know for sure is that I'm not sitting in the middle. I don't want half of the plane on its way to New York while the half I'm in is dropping down on Baltimore.

Turn Right at K-Mart

Another major airline, one of the country's best, in one week had a flight land at the wrong airport, had a near-miss (why don't they call it a near-hit?) over Newfoundland, had a flight land on the wrong runway, and had yet another take off without clearance. I had to know the facts, so I bribed an official with the airline to give me the inside scoop.

"So, tell me," I began, "how do you explain a plane landing in Frankfort, Kentucky, when it was supposed to be landing in Lexington?"

"Picky, picky, picky," said my source. "At least we got the right state. Plus, it was night and the crew couldn't look out the window and find the K-Mart where they're supposed to hang a right when they are landing in Lexington."

"Well, what about the near-miss when your plane was sixty miles off course?" I asked.

"I have talked with the pilots," my source continued, "and they said they were trying to dodge meteors. You never know where you'll run into a meteor shower."

I asked about the plane that landed on the wrong runway.

"It's bound to happen occasionally. Runways all look alike," he said. "They're long and narrow with a bunch of numbers on them. So you never turned up a one-way street before? It could happen to anybody."

"And the flight that took off without clearance?" I inquired.

"The press got that all wrong. We didn't take off without clearance. We took off without Clarence . . . Clarence Elrod, the navigator, who got lost on the way to the airport. Couldn't delay the flight waiting on him, you know."

Bring Your Own Air

At the same time the airlines are experiencing more problems, they're cutting back service to their customers. As usual, the consumer gets it on both ends.

Just last week I called to make reservations. Here's how the conversation went:

"Good morning, Treetop Airlines. May I help you?"

"Yes," I said, "I'd like to make two round-trip reservations for the Sunday evening flight to Pittsburgh."

"Will this be first-class, tourist, or Treetop's new cargo class?"

"Cargo class?"

"Certainly, sir. In an effort to attract your business in these competitive times, Treetop Airlines is offering an innovative and inexpensive way for you to travel by air. Cargo class simply means you ride in the cargo hold with the baggage at a huge savings in cost. There are certain restrictions on this fare, however, such as you must be able to fit inside your luggage, and there is no smoking in the cargo hold."

"I'll just take tourist," I said.

"Oxygen or non-oxygen?"

"I don't understand."

"It's another Treetop Airlines option in our effort to offer passengers a variety of ways to save money and still not have to take the bus," she explained. "If you prefer to bring your own oxygen tank, then your seat will not be equipped with an automatic oxygen mask release in case of sudden cabin depressurization. If Treetop doesn't have to provide you with oxygen, it can save money and pass those savings along to its customers in the form of reduced fares to places you're not likely ever to want to go."

"But I don't have my own oxygen tank."

"In that case, sir, how long can you hold your breath?"

"I'll just take two seats with oxygen."

"Will you be traveling with your wife or another adult?"

"No, I'll be traveling with my godson Robert, who's six."

"Does he chew Rootie-Tootie bubble gum?"

"Is that the kind that turns his teeth blue?" I asked.

"Exactly, sir, and Treetop Airlines now offers free tickets to children if they show eight Rootie-Tootie bubble-gum

wrappers when they go to the agent for their boarding passes. 'Get 'em while they're young and they're yours forever!' is what we always say at Treetop Airlines,'' she explained.

"So what is the adult fare?''

"Depends, sir, on your choice of seats. If you're willing to sit between two overweight people, your fare can be reduced by a third. If you're willing to sit next to a person who hasn't bathed in a week, you can save up to one-half on your normal fare.''

"I believe I'll just pay the full price. Now, this is a dinner flight, isn't it?''

"Not in tourist, sir. Treetop Airlines lost millions last year, and in an effort to keep our costs down, we have cut out all meal service except in first-class, where passengers are allowed to bob for apples.''

Where is Ralph Nader when you need him?

Carry on, Jethro

Judging from the amount of luggage most people haul onto planes these days, one of the cost-saving cutbacks must have been checked baggage. Every time I fly, I see at least one birdbrain walking onto the plane with enough baggage to send a grown mule to its knees.

I've had my bags sent to Caracas when I was going to Charleston, too, but that doesn't mean I want to keep my suitcases with me at all times.

These carry-on freaks haul huge hang-up bags, suitcases, briefcases, and their companies' entire computer systems. First they try to walk down the aisle without decapitating other passengers; then they attempt to put what obviously wouldn't fit into a Ryder truck into one of those tiny overhead compartments. At the end of the flight they open the compartment doors and act surprised as the

contents crash onto the heads of those below.

I fully expect to see somebody get on an airplane one of these days with a crate full of live chickens and a goat on a rope. It'll be like riding on the back of Jed Clampett's truck with Jethro Bodine.

Whining Won't Help

It's interesting to me that most advances in aviation can be traced to the military, where the favorite saying is "Hurry up and wait." That motto should be carved in stone outside every airport.

One week not long ago I flew every day—seven straight days of sober terror or drunken stupor—and every flight was late leaving and late arriving. On one flight from Dallas/Fort Worth to Las Vegas, we taxied out to the runway only to discover that some bozo who wanted to go to El Paso had gotten on the wrong plane. Back to the terminal and a one-hour delay.

Another time there was a mechanical problem—something about they couldn't get the engines started. I asked a stewardess for an explanation, and she said they were going to do something similar to jump-starting a car. Oh, my God! All I could think of was Bubba with a pair of jumper cables.

A couple of flights were oversold, and we spent half an hour auctioning off free tickets on future flights for anyone who would give up a seat. Another day we sat on the runway for nearly two hours waiting for a lightning storm to pass. Now, I'm all for yielding to lightning, but two hours on an airplane that won't fly is like being trapped in a phone booth all day without change.

The worst of all, however, was . . . well, fortunately I got the whole thing on tape. Otherwise, you'd think I made it up:

"Ladies and gentlemen, welcome aboard Air Delay flight 333 to Denver. Our flying time to the Mile High City today will be approximately two hours and forty-five minutes. Do not let that lull you into a false sense of security that we will arrive at our destination anywhere near on time, however.

"Due to heavy traffic here at the airport at this time, we are presently 108th in line for takeoff, which means we are going to spend approximately the next four hours and ten minutes either taxiing out or simply sitting still in the middle of a lot of other airplanes, waiting our turn to take off.

"Air Delay would like to apologize for this inconvenience. We realize that some of you have connections or important meetings in Denver today and that this little delay may cause you to lose your company's top client, among other disastrous possibilities.

"But please do not whine because we cannot help it if thirty-five other airlines decided to schedule takeoffs at exactly the same time we did.

"We will do everything in our power to make up for this excruciating experience. For those of you who might want to read while we are taxiing out, ask your flight attendant to bring you something from the Air Delay in-flight library. Available today are *War and Peace, The Rise and Fall of the Third Reich,* and *The Complete Works of Victor Hugo.*

"Later in our taxi out, we will be offering our regular Air Delay movie-while-you-wait. Our feature in first-class today is the uncut version of *Gone with the Wind,* while our coach passengers will enjoy viewing *Rocky I, Rocky II,* and *Rocky III.*

"If we still haven't taken off by the time the movies are over, then Air Delay has other means of killing time for our passengers. There will be a bridge tournament in rows twenty-five through thirty. For those who prefer bingo, cards may be purchased for a nominal charge. First

Officer Willard Smith, who is just as bored as you are, will be calling the game in rows seven through twenty-four.

"In first-class there will be Trivial Pursuit games and mud wrestling for any passengers who are interested, as well as a musical performance by two of our flight attendants, Ramona Dentz and Glenda Jane Chastain. They'll be singing songs they actually wrote themselves, such as 'I've Got the Air Sickness Bag Blues.'

"Other pre-takeoff performances include a lecture by Captain Allis Chalmers, who will explain how to hot-wire a Boeing 747, and a demonstration on in-flight macramé by navigator Marco Polonski.

"Also, because of the long delay, our smoking passengers may step outside to smoke. Please remember, however, to walk along with the aircraft in case it moves so that you don't get too far behind.

"Thank you, and have a pleasant flight."

Cough It Up, Buddy

The new Federal Aviation Administration directives on smoking have made air travel even more difficult for a lot of people—no smoking on flights that last less than two hours. (I wonder if that applies to flying time alone or flying and waiting time?) In California, they have banned smoking on all commercial flights.

These new directives led my friend Rigsby, ever the entrepreneur, to come up with a bold new business idea.

"I'm going to lease some airplanes and start a new airline for smokers only," said Rigsby. "You can smoke all you want on my planes. In fact, I will encourage smoking.

"Flight attendants will carry cigarettes up and down the aisles like the girls in Vegas. I'll charge five bucks a pack. A smoker who runs out of cigarettes on an airplane is a desperate individual who'll pay anything for another pack," he explained.

"So what are you going to call this new airline?" I asked.

"I've got my marketing staff working on that now," he said. "We're thinking of something that will really catch the smoking public's attention, something like Black Lung Airlines. Or maybe Air Emphysema."

I suggested they keep working on the name a little longer.

"OK," said Rigsby, "so we haven't found the perfect name yet, but let me tell you what else I'm going to offer on my all-smokers airline. First, we're going to make certain that no non-smokers come aboard and harass our customers. We will check each passenger's teeth and fingers. If they aren't yellow with tobacco stains, they don't get a boarding pass.

"We're not going to fly high enough to need cabin

pressurization, so our passengers won't have to worry about ever having to use those oxygen masks and not being able to smoke.

"Our flight crew will be all smokers, as well as our flight attendants, mechanics, reservationists and boarding agents. We'll have cigarettes going all the time. Nobody will ever have to ask for a light."

"Well," I asked, "won't it get pretty smoky on the plane with everybody puffing?"

"No problem," said Rigsby. "We're going to issue a miner's hat with the little light on the front so passengers can find their way to the lavatories."

"When will your advertising campaign begin?"

"Very soon," he said, "and it's going to be an award-winning campaign. Our slogan is 'An all-smokers airline—here to serve you just in the nick of teen.' Catchy, huh?"

May I Be Excused?

I'm always goofing up when I fly. Sometimes I forget to bring my seat back to its original and upright position for takeoffs and landings. Sometimes I forget to hand my trash to the stewardesses as they pass up and down the aisles.

Probably the worst thing I do when I fly, however, is in the unlikely event there is a loss of cabin pressure, I don't breathe normally when I place the oxygen mask over my head and face. I breathe like Secretariat down the stretch.

The other day, I goofed up something new.

I boarded the flight a few minutes before it was scheduled to take off and then sat there waiting for forty minutes. After sitting without moving for that long, I had to go to the bathroom.

I was inside the bathroom for maybe eleven seconds

when there was a loud banging on the door.

"Sir! Sir!" cried a female voice, obviously that of one of the flight attendants. "We can't pull back from the gate while you're in there. You're holding up the flight."

We've been sitting for forty minutes without so much as flapping our wings, and now we can't wait another couple of seconds for me to answer Mother Nature's call?

I hurried as much as I could, which meant wet stains down the front of my pants, and returned to my seat. All up and down the aisle passengers stared at me and whispered things like "Nice going, weak-bladder."

After we were airborne, the flight attendant brought me a computer printout of the rule requiring everyone to be in his or her seat before the plane pulls back from the gate. (It was right before rule 13A, which required at least one crying baby on every domestic flight.) She wanted me to know that she was just doing her job.

Maybe so, but what could this lead to? Will we have to start raising our hands to go to the bathroom anytime the plane is on the ground?

"OK, 14B," the flight attendant might say, "you can be excused but make it snappy."

Some things can't be accomplished snappily, especially if there is the added pressure that one might be holding up an entire L-1011.

Besides, the airlines would probably just use it as another excuse for being late: "Sorry, folks," the pilot could say. "We could have been on time if the guy in 14B had gone to the bathroom before he left home."

A Mixed Bag of Nuts

I must admit that I have met some interesting people on planes. Once during another hour-long wait at the gate, a woman sitting beside me started crying.

"Something wrong?" I asked gallantly.

"It took me a year to get up the courage to leave my boyfriend and start a new life for myself somewhere else," she sobbed. "If this thing doesn't take off soon, I'm afraid I'll chicken out and won't go."

Another time I sat next to a religious nut.

"Brother," he said to me, "do you know the Lord?"

I said I knew *of* Him.

"Are you ready to meet Him?" he continued.

I looked out the window. We were at twenty thousand

feet and climbing.

"I thought this was the Milwaukee flight," I said.

I was on a nonstop flight from Atlanta to Los Angeles. The fellow sitting next to me said, "Going to Los Angeles?"

"I hope so," I answered. "I really hope so."

Once on a flight that wasn't very crowded, I got into a lengthy conversation with a stewardess. She told me she had recently ended a five-year relationship with a pilot.

"I'll never forget the day we broke up," she said. "He called me from the airport, just before takeoff. We had an awful fight and I hung up on him."

"Was he mad?" I asked.

"Was he mad? He pulled the plane away from the gate and rammed one of the wings into another plane. He was always one to pout."

A pouting pilot. I think I'm going to be sick.

Did Somebody Say Oops?

I have logged more air miles in recent years than most pilots. One airline tried to get me to cash in my frequent-flyer points for a DC-10 of my own. I told them to keep it.

But despite all those miles and the fact that I'm still here, uncharred and with all my parts, I'm still afraid of flying. It just ain't natural.

Every time I get on a plane, I remember a picture I once saw on a pilot's wall. It was a photograph of an airplane that had crashed headlong into a tree and was suspended by the branches.

Under the photograph were these words: "Aviation itself is inherently safe, but in many ways it can be less forgiving of human error than the sea."

I understand human error—I've made a few myself—but I don't like hearing the words "Oops!" or "I forgot to . . ." at thirty thousand feet.

I prefer to envision John Wayne or Robert Stack behind the controls, and if their minds wander at all from their work, I want them thinking about a gorgeous woman waiting for them on the ground. What we get too often, however, is final words from a black box like, "Hey, did you see the wazoos on that woman in 23C? Oops!"

But I still have to fly if I want to work in this profession . . . and it's the only one I know. So I do whatever I can to make flying less frightening. Here are a few tips that I've found helpful:

1. I tend to drink a lot before getting on a plane. I'm not talking about a shooter or two. I'm talking about going to the Crown Room a day before my flight and drinking double screwdrivers until they scrape me up and load me onto one of those buggies that carry handi-

capped people.

2. I tend to drink a lot while I'm in the air. The only resulting problem is that sometimes when the plane lands, I get off and can't remember what city I was traveling to. So I ask where I am, but then I can't remember what I was supposed to do when I got there. So I go to the Crown Room and start getting ready for the flight home.

3. When I have a choice, I prefer to fly with the airline that has had the most recent crash. I figure the odds are in my favor.

4. I never fly on the national airlines of Communist countries or those of countries where they wear sheets or think cows are sacred.

5. I never fly on commuter airlines. If the pilots were any good, they'd be flying for a *real* airline instead of a puddle-jumper.

6. I take along a good book to keep my mind off the

dangers. I suggest this one.

7. I call the home of the pilot the night before takeoff to make certain that he isn't drinking and that he's in bed early. If I suspect there's any tension with a wife or girlfriend, I send him flowers with mash notes.

8. I never eat the food they serve on-board. That way I never have to loosen my grip on the seat.

9. I discourage casual conversation with those sitting around me so that I can listen more closely for changes in the sound of the engines.

10. I pray a lot. I've always heard there are no atheists in foxholes. I doubt there are any in a 727 that is passing through a serious storm after taking off from Boston at night. I also try not to think any dirty thoughts on an airplane so God will like me and listen to my prayers.

Happy vapor trails to you.